WRITING POETRY:
AS EASY AS 1-2-3

WRITING POETRY:
AS EASY AS 1-2-3

GEORGETTE G. LEE

TABLE OF CONTENTS

Dedication 7

Introduction..8

1. The One-Line Poem...10

2. The Couplet..14

3. The Tercet..18

     Poetic Triplet 19

     Terza Rima 20

     The Haiku 21

4. The Quatrain...22

5. The Cinquain..26

     The Reverse Cinquain 29

     The Limerick 30

     Sensory Poem 33

6. The Sestet..36

7. The Septet..42

     The Diamante 43

     Synonym Diamante 44

     Antonym Diamante 47

8. The Octave 50

9. The Spenserian Stanza...54

10. The Decastich..58

11. The Roundel..62

12. The 12-Line Poem...66

13. The Thirteen Line Poem 70

14. The Sonnet 74

About the Author...82

DEDICATION

This book is dedicated to my students who daily open their minds to the ease and beauty of poetry, in realizing that poetry is within each of us just waiting to be unleashed.

INTRODUCTION

"Writing Poetry: As Easy as One-Two-Three" is a line-by-line guide to writing poetry. It was conceptualized out of a desire to teach my students the ease of which poetry can be written. In delivering an introductory unit on poetry to commemorate National Poetry Month at the middle school where I work, I came up with the concept of presenting poetry in numeric lines. After each lesson, in every class, all students produced a beautiful poem. Many students were amazed at their creativity, and the teachers were excited about the students' engagement and productivity. Everyone came away with the idea that poetry can be as easy as counting one-two-three.

Even though the poems in this book were used with middle school students, this collection is so versatile as to be engaging for younger and older readers. Teachers and parents alike can use it as a resource for introducing younger students to writing a variety of poems, while the more seasoned poet can broaden his or her experiences with poetry.

A poem begins (and ends) with a single line, and expands into a countless number of lines. Each group of lines is a specific type of poem with its unique rules and structure. In this book, I explore poetry writing; starting with the one-line poem and continuing in numeric order to a variety of multi-lines poems, including the ageless favorites like Haikus, Limericks, and Sonnets. Let's count and let's write poetry together. Be assured, It's as easy as counting 1-2-3!

CHAPTER 1

The One-Line Poem

A poem is made up of a grouping of lines called a stanza. It begins with the first word, the first line. Did you know that some lines are so profound, so pregnant with meaning that they stand as poetry on their own? This one line is the building block for all poetry. To begin, think of describing something, an idea, an event, or a situation, using eight to twelve syllables:

"Sweltering heat, bodies bleeding sweat, smelling burnt"

What image does this poem conjure up? I was describing a day at a down-town parade with temperatures exceeding ninety degrees. For dramatic effect, you can use literary devices such as alliteration, metaphor, or simile.

Writing poetry is as easy as one, two, three.

Mango pineapple smoothie, pure delight!

Hush, let silence speak its profound wisdom.

Listen carefully, hear these hollow eyes weep.

Touch creativity in these rough, scarred hands.

Diamond-rough hands, nothing to show but cracks and creases.

Rumbling, tumbling weather, crouched under covers.

Magical, mouth-making, mesmerizing music!

CHAPTER 2

The Couplet

The couplet is a two-line poem that rhymes (Two lines that rhyme). The lines must have the same number of syllables and express a complete thought. Like the one-line poem, the couplet may be extended to form a longer poem. Couplets may be funny or serious. When words rhyme in a poem, they share the same letter, starting with the letter "a". The couplet has an "aa" rhyming pattern.

<u>Couplet</u>
A couplet is a pair
A single thought they share

<u>Love</u>
Oh love, forever pure, so divine
Tightly join my lover's heart and mine

<u>Time</u>
Oh time, be kind, I want for you to stay
Why must you pass so quickly on your way?

In this poem, "Summer Fun," I have combined three couplets:

<u>Summer Fun</u>
Summer is here, let the fun begin
Step in the water up to my chin

Go under waves, waddle and wade
Then relax with drinks beneath the shade

Read a great book and sing a sweet song
Enjoy life before fall comes along

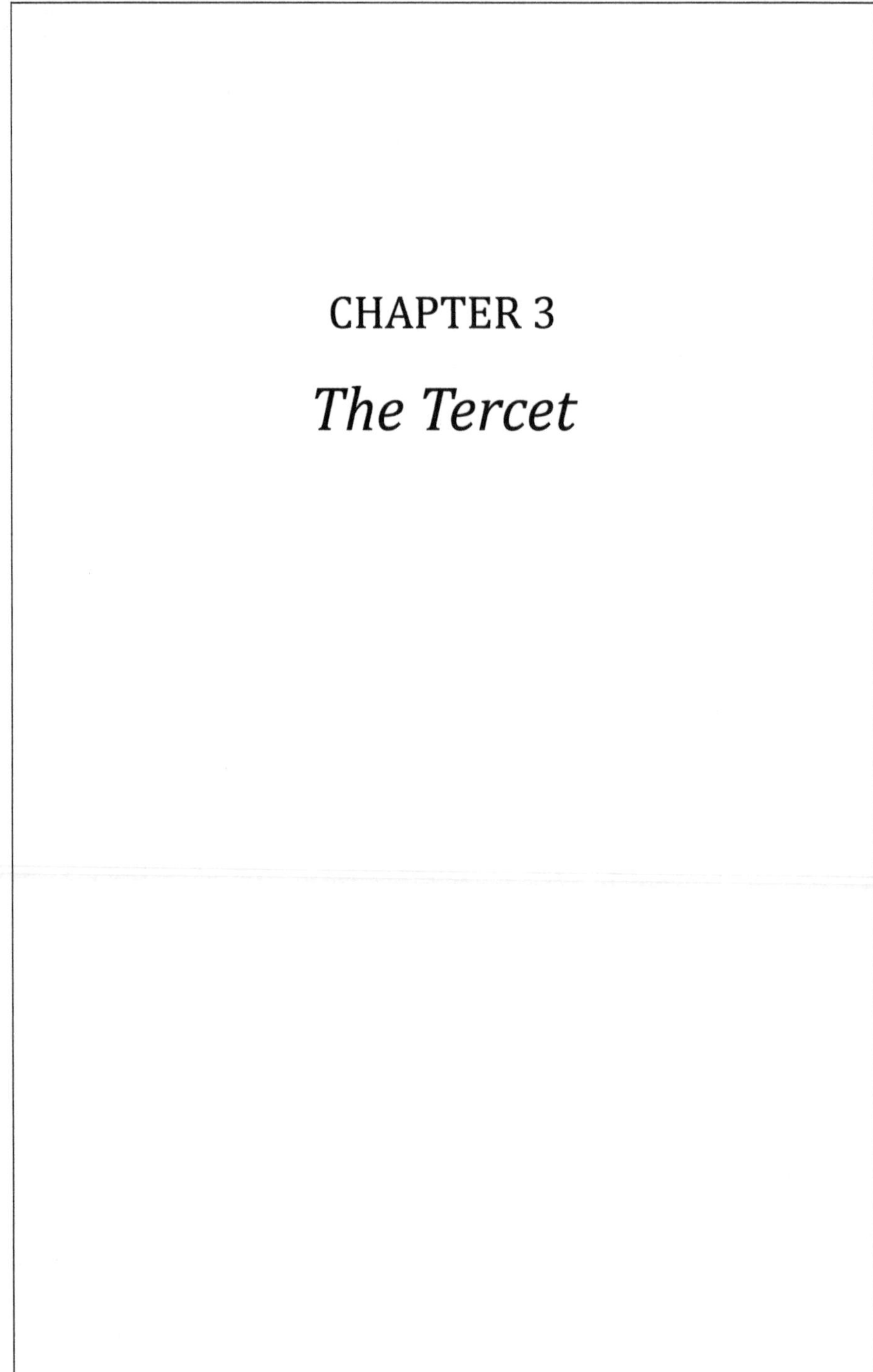

CHAPTER 3

The Tercet

The Tercet is made up of three lines forming a stanza or complete poem. It expresses a single thought, and, like the Couplet, each line has an equal number of syllables. There are many variations of Tercets. The poetic Triplet is a Tercet in which all three lines follow the same rhyming scheme or pattern—**"aaa."**

Wearily walking home
Passing under the dome
No other place to roam

I'm happy that school's in
Studies will now begin
Create, think, imagine!

Another kind of Tercet is the enclosed Tercet where the lines follow an **"aba"** rhyming pattern:

The hungry cat
Peeps through the hole
Baiting the rat

Mix spring showers
And sunlight to
Make bright flowers

Terza Rima

Yet another poetic form made up of the Tercet is called the **Terza Rima**. In this poem, the "aba" rhyming pattern of the first stanza is repeated in the following stanza, by making the two outer lines (Lines 1 and 3) rhyme with the middle line (Line 2) of the previous stanza (bcb).

SPRING BREAK

Getting away is always fun,
Time to rest, relax, and play,
Securing a break from "on the run."

~ ~ ~

Enjoying this sunny day,
Complementary breakfast, indoor pool,
How I relish this time of year.

~ ~ ~

Hanging out with friends is cool,
To the mall, brunch, then a movie,
Spring break—number one rule.

~ ~ ~

The Haiku

The haiku is a special type of three-line poem. Originally from Japan, it is made of seventeen syllables (5-7-5 syllable pattern). The traditional haiku is usually about nature, but English haiku may be about any topic. Use lots of sensory description (sight, taste, touch, sound, and scent), and be objective (No use of "I").

Starlight sprinkled 'ore
the sky, painting pictures of
brilliant beauty.
~~~~~~~~
Summer rains falling
softly, ridding the day of
its tortuous heat!
~~~~~~~~
Tears of happiness
flowing rapidly down this
face of victory.

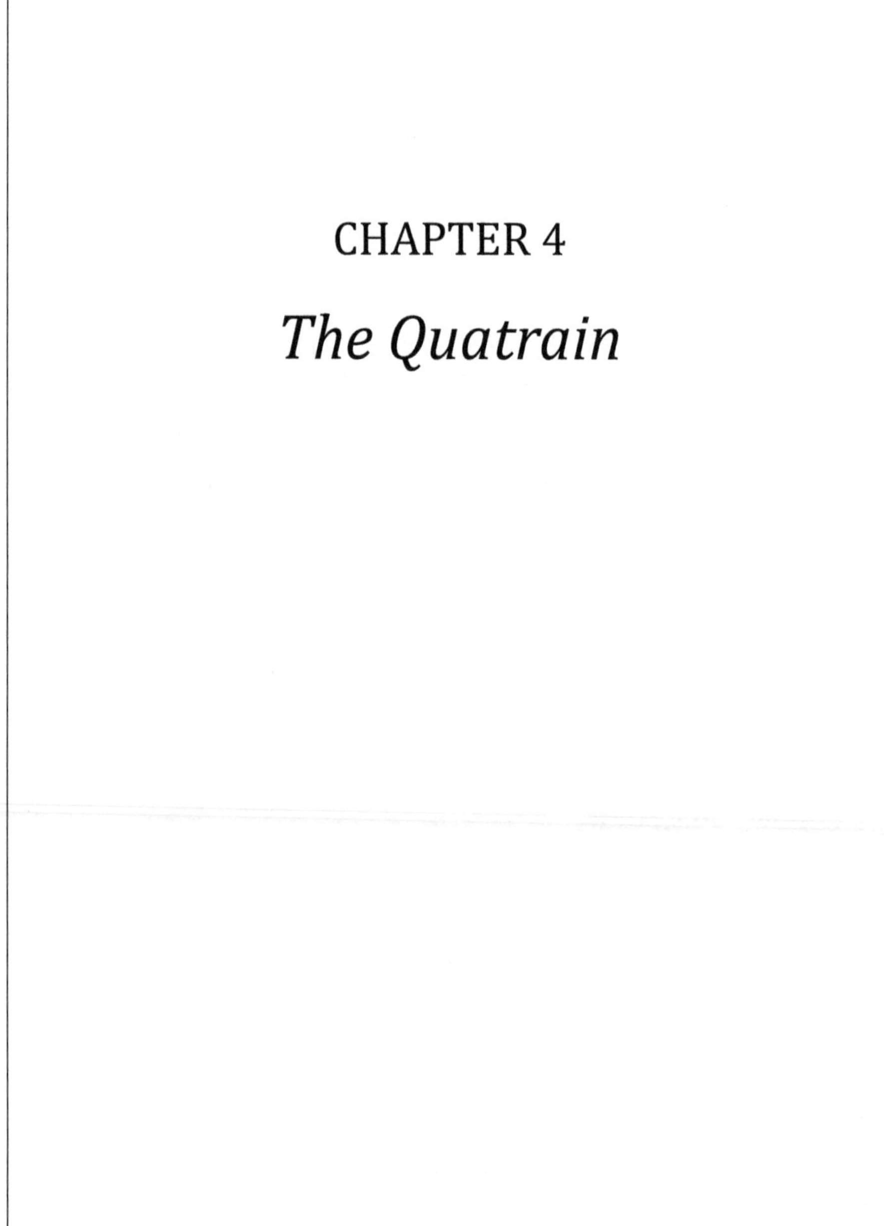

CHAPTER 4

The Quatrain

The Quatrain may be the most common form of poetry. It is made up of four lines, each line having an equal number of syllables. This poem has a variety of rhyming patterns, including aaaa (all four lines rhyme); abab (Line 1 rhymes with Line 3, and Line 2 rhymes with Line 4); and aabb (Line 1 and 2 rhyme, and Lines 3 and 4 rhyme). The first poem I remember writing started as a Quatrain, and went on to have eleven stanzas of quatrains. I've lost this poem over the years, but vividly remember the first Stanza.

<u>My favorite Card</u>
My favorite card is a Birthday card
That was given to me by my mother
It has a caption at the top that reads
"Happy Birthday to my Charming Daughter."

There's a picture of a huge rose bouquet
That covers the card and such beauty shows
It is sprinkled with coarse, glitter-like beads
That sparkle with luster as the light glows.

Though the years have faded my birthday card
And mom has gone to her heavenly rest
Other celebratory cards do come
But this remains the card I love the best.

<u>Holiday Season</u>

It's snowing, it's snowing,
Scented candles are glowing,
I don't have to worry,
Going nowhere in a hurry.

~~~~~

My family is here
Gathered 'round me today,
Sharing joy and happiness,
This season of cheer and bliss.

~~~~~

Reading cards, opening gifts,
Checking items off my list,
Feeling sentimental though,
Missing those gone on before.

~~~~~

Decked hall, boughs of holly
Make the season fun and jolly,
Thankful for another year,
And the love you freely share.
~~~~~

CHAPTER 5

The Cinquain

The Cinquain is a five-line poem. Its name is derived from the French word "cinq" which means "Five". There are many variations of Cinquain poetry, but the one used most often in schools and for beginning poets is called the Didactic Cinquain. Word count (not syllables) is important in this type of poem. The first line is a one-word title which is the subject of the poem. The second line is a pair of adjectives describing that title; the third line is a three-word phrase that gives more information about the subject; the fourth line is made up of four words that describe feelings/emotions related to the subject; while the fifth line is a single word synonym or other reference for the subject used in line one.

Title (One word)
Two Adjectives describing the title (Two words)
Three-word phrase with more information about the title (Three words)
Four words describing feelings about the title (Four words)
Synonym for subject in line one (One word)

Writing
Relaxing, Aesthetic
Thought-provoking activity
Reveals your deepest emotions
Expression

Poetry
Limerick, Cinquain
Rhythm of life
Deliriously happy, Dejectedly sad
Verse

The Reverse Cinquain

Another form of Cinquain is called the Reverse Cinquain. Instead of counting words, this form counts syllables and follows a 2, 8, 6, 4, 6 syllable pattern.

Mother
Loving, Caring, Resilient
Sturdy bearer of life
Eternal bond
Lover, Nurturer, Friend

. . . .

Teacher
Enjoys nurturing her students
Pinnacle of Knowledge
Educator
Caring, Understanding.

The Limerick

Another five-line poem is the Limerick. It is a funny, nonsense poem with a special rhyming pattern and rhythm (or beat). The last word of Lines 1, 2, and 5 rhyme with each other; while the last word of Lines 3 and 4 rhyme with each other. We call the rhyming words in Lines 1, 2, and 5 "**a**," and the rhyming words from Lines 3 and 4 "**b**". The rhyming pattern is "aabba".

To create the special rhythm of the Limerick, the first, second, and fifth lines have 8 to 10 syllables each. The third and fourth lines each have a 5 to 7 syllable beat.

<u>Dirty Drew</u>
There once was a bad girl named Drew
Who spilled juice on top of her shoe
Though it made her mom mad
Drew always seemed glad
To shine her one shoe until new

. . . .

<u>Cowardly Tim</u>

There once was a fellow named Tim

Whose outlook on life seemed so grim

He refused to shower

From all he would cower

The last time we ever saw him

. . . .

<u>Lady Lisle</u>

There was an old lady called Lisle

Who enticed a large crocodile

To cross over the lake

A large cake she would bake

And feed to the croc with a smile

. . . .

<u>SECRETIVE JACK</u>

There once was a young boy called Jack
Who wore a huge bag on his back
He seemed in no hurry
To divulge his story
Of what lurked inside of that pack

. . . .

<u>ODD COUPLE</u>

There was a young girl from Bim
Who was decidedly thin
She went on a date
With a guy overweight
And fell madly in love with him

Sensory Poem

The Sensory poem in its most basic form is another type of five-line poetry. Each line uses one of the senses. The lines do not have to rhyme. This poem is very versatile, and may be used to express feelings about an object, idea, person, or experience. Note that the senses may be presented in any order.

Mango
I SEE your ripened, golden yellow skin
I FEEL invigorated as I anticipate the delight of having you
I SMELL your distinctive, inviting aroma that screams "Take me!"
I TASTE your succulent, mouth-watering juices
I HEAR my lips smack with every swallow of my delicious mango

AT HOME
I SEE the sun set over your beautiful land
I HEAR the birds calling their loved-ones home to nest
I SMELL the sea sprays mixing with the white sand
I TASTE the salty air sitting on my luscious lips
I FEEL completely relaxed on my island home—Barbados

<u>INTERVIEW</u>

I SEE the opposing candidates smartly dressed

I SMELL in the office atmosphere a trail of success

I FEEL hesitant, yet excited about my prospects

I HEAR a voice summoning me to the inner chamber

I TASTE victory as I present my impressive portfolio

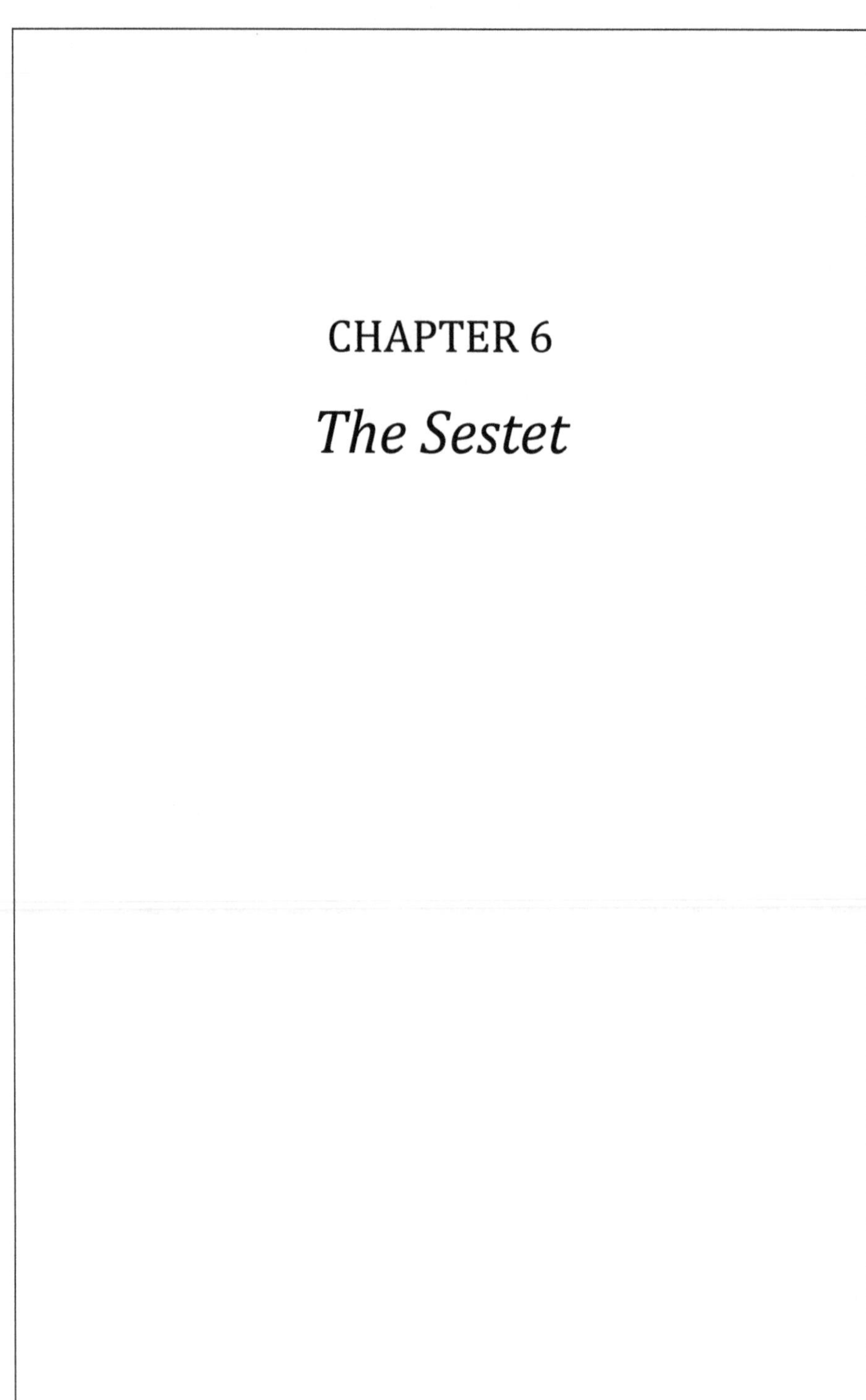

CHAPTER 6

The Sestet

The Sestet is a six-line poem. Sestets are one section of a fourteen-line poem called a Sonnet. But Sestets can stand alone. Triplets can easily be doubled to create a Sestet. The following "New Year" poem is made up of a double sestet:

<u>NEW YEAR</u>
Brand new day, new morn,
New sunrise, new dawn,
New inspiration is born.
New hopes, new dreams,
New visions, new schemes,
New pals, new teams.

. . . .

New race, new start,
New joy, new heart,
New love, never part.
New life, new year,
New start, never fear,
Good times—here to stay!

The <u>I AM Poem</u> is a fun poem made up of three successive stanzas of sestets. Create sentences about your feelings, hopes, dreams, and expectations to accompany the initial clue for each line.

I am
I wonder
I hear
I see
I want
I am

<u>STANZA 11</u>
I pretend
I feel
I touch
I worry
I cry
I am

<u>STANZA 111</u>

I understand

I say

I dream

I try

I hope

I am

. . . .

I am dedicated and persistent

I wonder why we grow old

I hear my mom praying for me

I see a beautiful future ahead

I want an end to war

I am creative

. . . .

I **pretend** that I'm superhuman
I **feel** satisfied with where I am
I **touch** the lives of children
I **worry** about violence in schools
I **cry for** children who lose their lives aimlessly
I **am** caring

. . . .

I **understand** that Rome wasn't built in a day
I **say** encouraging words
I **dream** the impossible
I **try** to do my best always
I **hope** for a better tomorrow
I **am** an optimist

. . . .

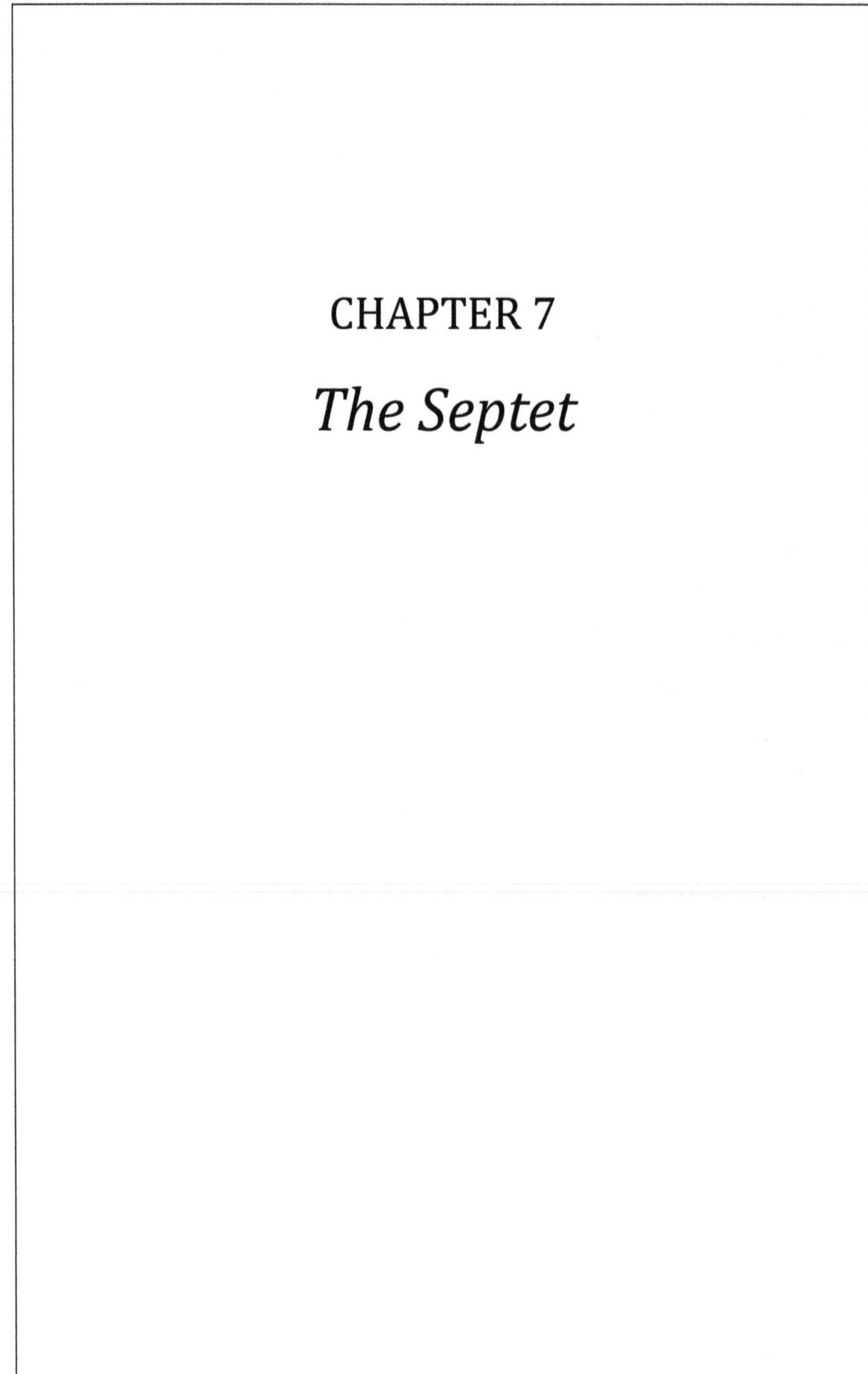

CHAPTER 7

The Septet

A seven-line poem is called a Septet. There are different forms of Septets but a funny, familiar one is the Diamante.

The Diamante

The Diamante poem is made up of seven lines in the form of a diamond. It does not have to rhyme, but each line uses specific types of words such as adjectives, -ing verbs, synonyms, and antonyms. There are basically two types of Diamante poems—the **Synonym Diamante** and the **Antonym Diamante**. In the Synonym Diamante, the entire poem is based on a single topic or subject, while the Antonym Diamante is based on opposite subjects like winter and summer, day and night, or happy and sad.

Let's begin with the Synonym Diamante:

Line 1—**One** word (Topic/Subject)
Line 2—**Two Adjectives** about the topic
Line 3—**Three Verbs** ending in -ing related to the topic
Line 4—**Four Nouns** or short phrase about the topic
Line 5—**Three Verbs** ending in -ing related to the topic
Line 6—**Two Adjectives** about the topic
Line 7—**One** word to represent the topic

An easy way to write the Synonym Diamante is to begin with Line 1 and 7 (The topic of the poem and its corresponding synonym) and then fill in the remaining lines.

Pets

Cuddly, Cunning

Jumping, Fetching, Playing

Companion, Best Friend, Pal, Chum

Barking, Swimming, Licking

Funny, Faithful

Dogs

Fruits
Tasty, Healthful
Blending, Pulsing, Pealing
Mango Pineapple, Strawberry Banana
Shredding, Grating, Liquefying
Tart, Delicious
Smoothie

The format of the **Antonym Diamante** is as follows:

Line 1—**One** word (Topic/Subject)

Line 2—**Two Adjectives** about the topic

Line 3—**Three Verbs** ending in -ing related to the topic

Line 4—**Four Nouns** or short phrase about Lines 1 and 7

Line 5—**Three Verbs** ending in -ing about the topic of Line 7

Line 6—**Two Adjectives** about the topic of line 7

Line 7—**One** word opposite of topic in Line 1

It is easier to write the two parts (top and bottom) of the Antonym Diamante simultaneously. That is, write Lines 1 and 7; Lines 2 and 6; Lines 3 and 5; then finish the poem with Line 4 (half of which belongs to Line 1, and the other half to Line 7). There you have it!

Summer

Delightful, hot

Biking, Swimming, Traveling

The Longest days, The Longest nights

Decorating, Shivering, Caroling

Beautiful, Cold

Winter

. . . .

Night

Midnight, Secretive

Sleeping, Relaxing, Dreaming

Artificial light, Natural rays

Waking, Exercising, Working

Dawn, Revealing

Day

. . . .

Good

Positive, Comforting

Smiling, Loving, Helping

Cleave to the good, Refrain from evil

Frowning, Hating, Hindering

Negative, Disheartening

Evil

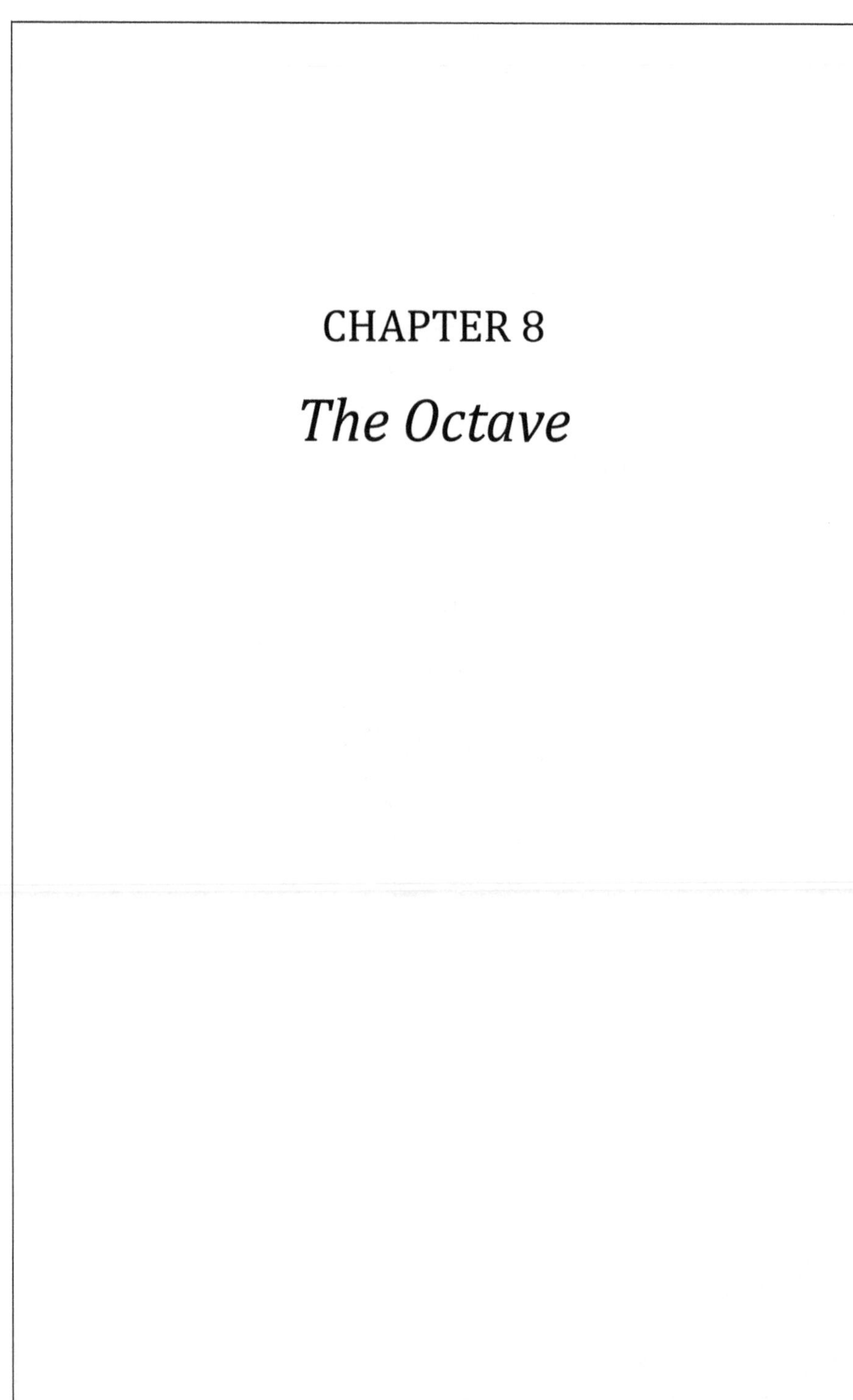

CHAPTER 8

The Octave

Octaves are eight-line poems. Octaves are also used for the first section of a Sonnet (which is a fourteen-line poem). One form of the Octave is the Ottava Rima which has an "abababcc" rhyming pattern. The lines are made of ten syllables (iambic pentameter). The lines of an Ottava Rima may also have eleven syllables (hendecasyllabic).

TEACHERS

Our greatest call is to serve each other,
Spreading seeds of knowledge where 'ere we go,
Being "best" is the crux of the matter,
Cultivating minds as we watch them grow,
Sharing our skills to make the world better,
Forever striving to stay in the know,
Making our mark on the world as teachers,
Though often scorned, we remain world leaders.

HOW MUCH DO I LOVE YOU?

How long will I love you? Let's count the ways:

I love you as long as the sky holds rain,

As long as hours keep turning to days,

As long as a mom's kiss erases pain,

As long as this breath in my body stays,

As long as "the Powers" our lives ordain.

I know that my heart will make no amends,

I love you until eternity ends.

CHAPTER 9

The Spenserian Stanza

The Spenserian Stanza is a form of poetry made up of nine lines. Each of the first eight lines has ten syllables (iambic pentameter), and the last line has twelve syllables (iambic hexameter) known as an Alexandrine. The Spenserian Stanza has an **"ababbcbcc"** rhyming scheme, and was named for the English poet Edmund Spenser (1552-1599). Of course, one can be less formal and juxtapose three Tercets to create a nine-line poem.

<u>STRETCHED TO THE LIMIT</u>
Just for the chance to stop and take a rest,
Body and soul pulled to the limit,
Time, delay a while to take my request,
Just a tiny break or else I plummet
Steadily downward to the lowest pit,
I seek mercy in some capacity,
The pressures of life rob me of my wit,
Chores, tasks, duties in multiplicity,
A chance to rest a while, unite diversity.

<u>Hope</u>

When night closes in it's best to have hope,
In spite of life's challenges don't give in,
For every new day brings fresh faith to cope,
With blessed assurance each moment begin
To utter prayers of repentance from sin.
No matter how low hope's flames may flicker,
Adorn yourself with an infectious grin,
Each disappointment makes your skin thicker,
Hope brings strength so you won't become bitter.

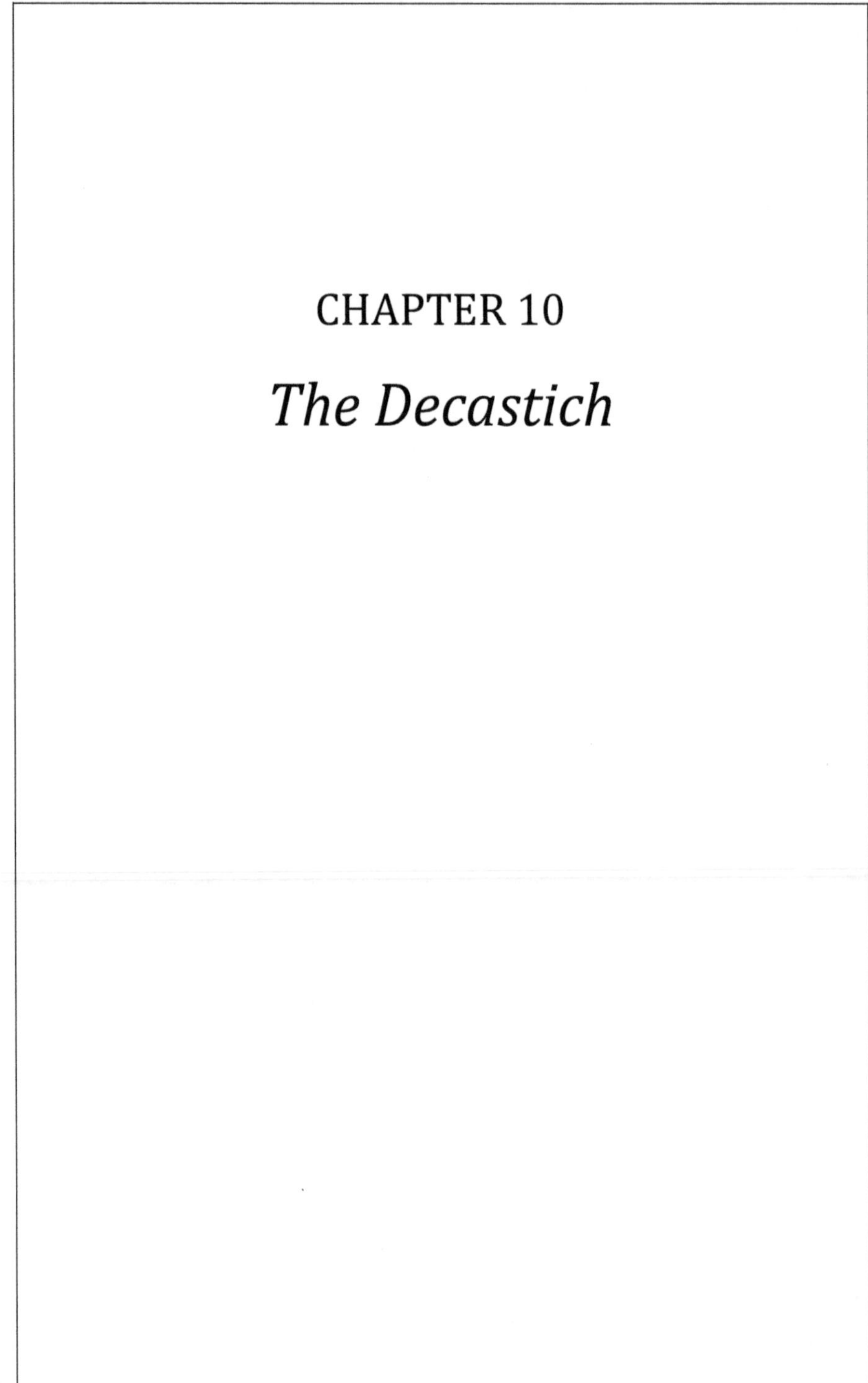

CHAPTER 10

The Decastich

A ten-line poem is called a Decastich. Its name was derived from the Greek prefix "deca" meaning "ten," and "sti'chos" meaning "line" or "row". The Decastich may be used with or without a rhyming pattern. The following poem, Jury Duty, is made up of three sets of Decastich.

<u>Jury Duty</u>
Doors open at eight-thirty, through the double doors,
By-pass the crowds at security, straight to the room for assembly,
At nine, the judge gives his speech of welcome, thanks to each
Of the potential jurors here, then he disappears.
The wait begins . . .
Read a book, take a cursory look at your surroundings,
Watch one of the three T.V. monitors,
But only the center one blurbs on and on, and on, and on . . . .
Then the door opens, and a man enters
With a list of names and numbers.

—

Listen, first name and juror numerals,
Doug, seventeen; Patricia, eighteen;
Clyde, twenty-one; Earl, eighty-three,
Still, no name nor number for me.
A group of thirty-five whistled away,
The remaining folks just sit there.
Tick-tock, tick-tock . . . another hour goes by,
Then another gentleman
repeats the routine of name and number,
Again, no reference to what's on my paper!

—

The wait continues . . . read a book, take a cursory look
At your surroundings,
Watch one of the three T.V. monitors,
But only the center one blurbs
On and on, and on, and on . . . .
Close the book, stop the cursory look at your surroundings,
Ignore the three T.V. monitors,
Notably the center one that blurbs on and on,
Then the door opens, and a man enters
And announces, "At this time, you may go home!"

CHAPTER 11

The Roundel

The Roundel is a form of eleven-line poetry, consisting of nine lines having the same number of syllables, and two refrains. The first line (or half of it) is repeated in lines four and eleven as a refrain. The refrain is identical to the beginning of the first line and rhymes with the second line. The Roundel has three stanzas with an **abaR**; **bab**; **abaR** rhyming pattern, with **R** being the refrain.

EMPOWERED

No longer Afraid, no longer saddened,
Your Word gives me the courage to break out
Of man's restricting mould, now I'm gladdened.
No longer Afraid! I've gone a new route!
Now time to spread my wings and dreams with clout,
Stretch wide my vision above this maddened
Crowd, raise my voice in a victory shout,
I've reached new horizons. Now unburdened,
Rid of limitations, free of self-doubt.
Hope for the hopeless, strength for the weakened
No longer afraid! I've gone a new route!

<u>Man On a Mission</u>

No time to waste, man is on a mission,
Restoring the faith in manly valor,
Duty calls, he answers the commission,
No time to waste, expending great labor.
Strong waves resisted, ships brought to harbor,
Fear now completely under submission,
Justice and fairness shall be his neighbor,
Climbing high, forming the coalition,
Forging on mightily, gaining power,
Placing man in his rightful position,
No time to waste, man becomes a savior.

CHAPTER 12

The 12-Line Poem

The longer the poem grows in lines, the less likely to find a specific term for the poem, or a set rhyming scheme. Twelve-line poems may or may not rhyme. You decide on your rhyming pattern. This poem may be attacked by grouping six Couplets, four Triplets, Three Quatrains, or two Sestets. Here's one with an "**aabbcccddeee**" rhyming pattern:

<u>Examination Anxiety</u>
For weeks, I labored on these paper trails,
Trying to recall your lectures' details
Focusing deeply on your every word
Each miniscule sound in class ever heard
Now, I see the examiner's questions
He must not make null my preparations
For these grueling examinations
No, my efforts can never be in vain
This blurry script must not bring me to shame
I pray to God from where strength is derived
The light of dawn has finally arrived
Another exam that I have survived!

This 12-Line poem was made with six couplets:

<u>Proud to be Me</u>
I'm proud to be me
Who else could I be?

The world needs my gifts
It cannot resist

No need to rival
For my survival,

No replication
No duplication

I'm one of a kind
And you should not mind

There's room for us all
Just answer your call.

RESILIENCE

You run from pillar to post spreading lies,

Trying to justify your vindictive actions,

But there is One who sees the heart,

He knows your motivations,

You try to exclude me by keeping me uninformed,

But it's not for long, my eyes are opened

To the ditches dug, contrived glitches.

He sets my feet on the rock, up high,

Above my woes and my foes.

And so I rise above the lies,

The deceit, the down-right bitchery,

For your actions bring out the best in me.

CHAPTER 13

The thirteen-line poetry has no special name, and no specific rhyming pattern, just a verse with thirteen lines.

<u>RESTRICTED</u>
Such restriction,
No motivation,
Can hardly move,
How long will you stay here
In frozen immobility,
Harnessed potentiality?
Let loose, let go,
Allow your thoughts to flow,
Your gains to grow,
Your soul to soar,
Sing your song,
How long? How Long
Before you learn, laugh, and LIVE?

I AM POETRY
I am words that dance magically
Off the page as voice renders me
Full of life, opportunities,
Your expert enunciation,
The rhythm, the beat
Release thoughts that make the broken-hearted weep,
Not tears of sadness, not of defeat,
But of infinite possibility,
For my words speak life, durability,
I speak of love and humanity,
Speak of meaning and form's inseparability,
Yes, you know me,
I am POETRY!

CHAPTER 14

The Sonnet

Probably the best known poetic form is the Sonnet, which is a fourteen-line poem that is divided into two sections. In the Italian Sonnet, the first section is an Octave (8-lines) followed by a Sestet (6-lines). Typically, the Octave raises a question that the Sestet answers. Sometimes, the two sections of the Sonnet show contrasting view points. The English Sonnet is made up of three quatrains (the conflict) and one couplet (the resolution). Originally, Sonnets spoke of love, but later, poets use sonnets to write about other topics such as politics and religion. There are numerous variations of Sonnets, each having its unique rhyming pattern.

The Court House

Tell me, why are you here today?
To stand on trial, or to be near
Someone to lend them your support,
To be a shelter, a strong fort?
Do you stand in the role of judge,
Perform your duties without grudge,
Or a lawyer for the defense,
A prosecutor who madly vents?
You too are a petit juror,
Here to do your civic duty,
Feeling just like a junior,
Perhaps a bit inferior,
Under the courtroom's scrutiny,
Yet, makes a sound verdict, super!

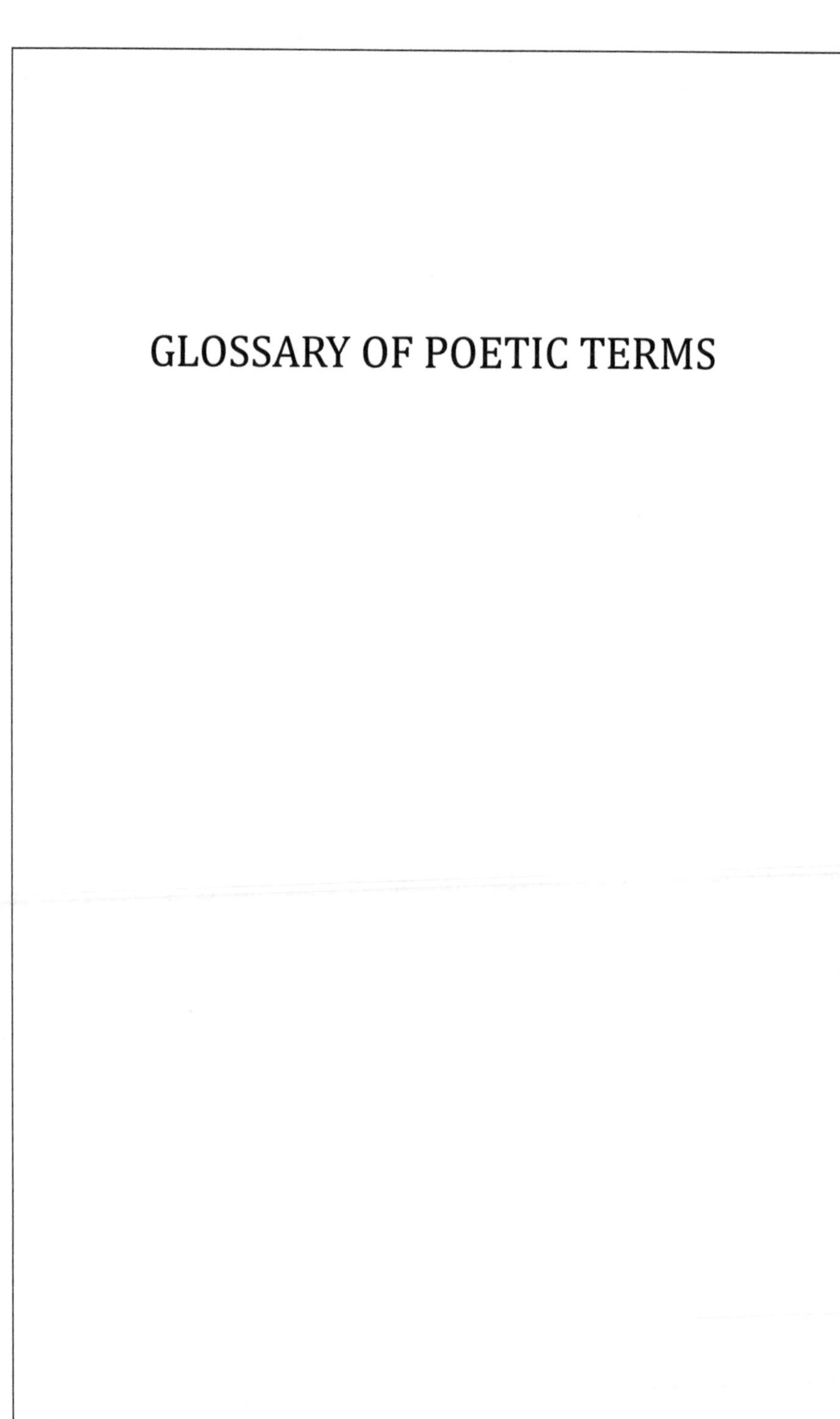

GLOSSARY OF POETIC TERMS

Antonym—A word that is opposite in meaning to another.

Cinquain—A class of poems with a five-line form that is defined by specific rules.

Couplet—A class of poems made up of two lines that rhyme and form a stanza or a complete poem.

Decastich—A class of poems comprised of ten lines.

Diamante—A class of seven-line poems that takes the shape of a diamond.

Haiku—A traditional Japanese verse, characterized by three respective lines of 5-7-5 syllables.

Limerick—A funny, witty form of five-line poems with a specific "aabba" rhyming pattern.

Octave—A class of poems comprised of eight lines; The first eight lines of an Italian Sonnet.

Poem—A composition in verse characterized by the creative use of language to express an idea or feeling of a subject.

Quatrain—A class of four-line poems forming a stanza or a complete poem.

Roundel—A class of eleven-line poems that uses refrains and has a specific rhyming scheme. The first nine lines have an equal number of syllables, plus a refrain after the third line, and after the last line.

Sensory poem—A poem that predominantly utilizes one or more of the senses (e.g., I see, I hear).

Septet—A class of seven-line poems having no particular for or meter.

Sestet—A class of six-line poems.

Sonnet—A class of fourteen-line poems, having a two-part structure comprised of a problem and a solution.

Spenserian Sonnet—A sonnet consisting of three Quatrains followed by a Couplet, with an interlocking rhyming pattern (abab, bcbc, cdcd, ee).

Stanza—A division of a poem made up of two or more line having a common pattern of meter, rhyme, and number of lines.

Synonym—A word that is similar in meaning to another.

Tercet—A class of three-line poems forming a stanza or a complete poem.

Terza Rima—A type of Tercet characterized by an interlocking rhyming pattern (aba, bcb, cdc).

Verse—A stanza of a poem.

ABOUT THE AUTHOR

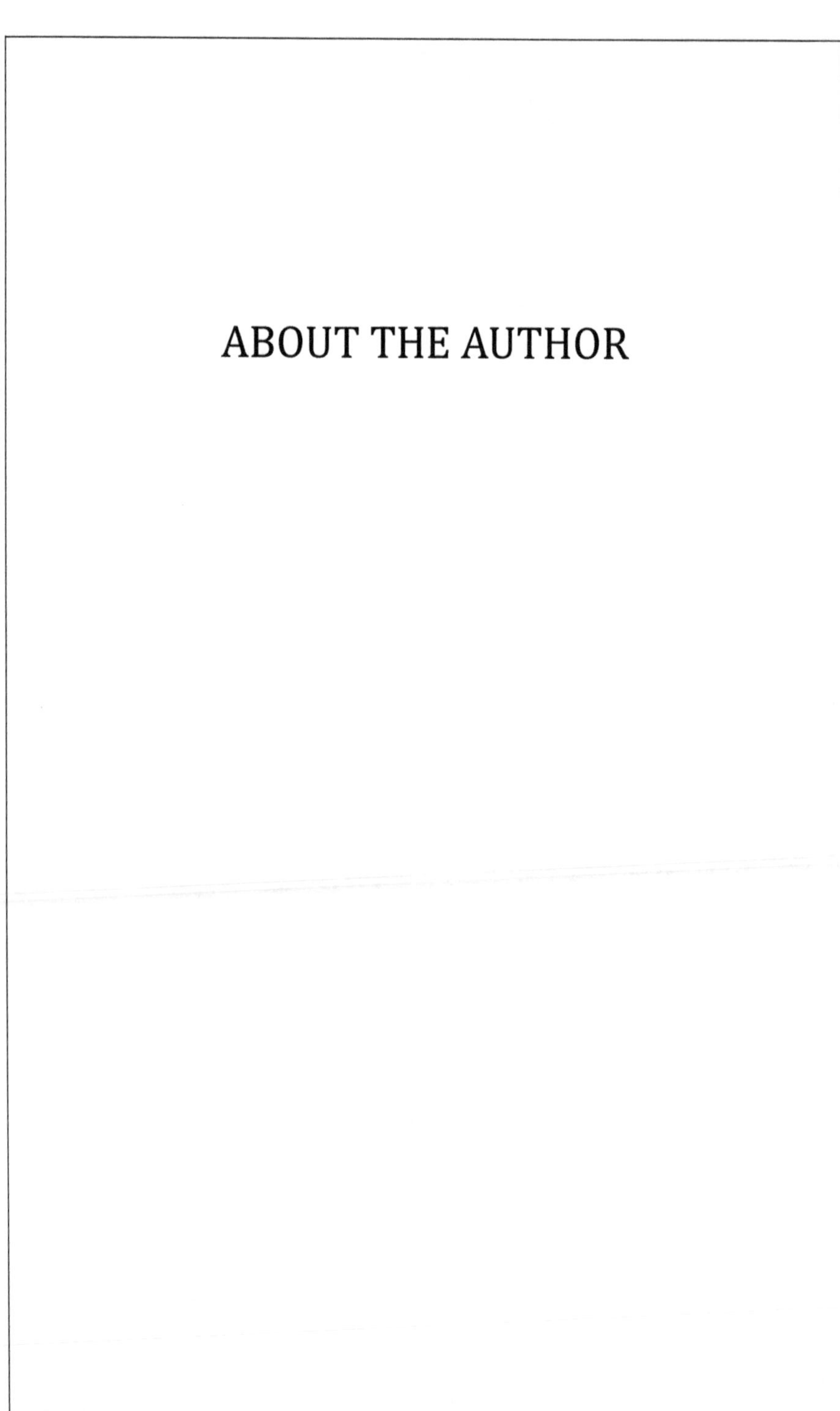

Dr. Georgette Lee is an avid poetry lover and writer. She is the author of two previous poetry collections, "Seasons," and "Poetically Speaking: Poems for the Elementary Classroom," and a memoir, "Layers of Living." Dr. Lee uses poetry to advance the literacy skills of her students, and has been instrumental in many of them publishing their personal poetry. When not writing, Dr. Lee enjoys gardening, traveling, and engaging in new craft projects. She gains her inspiration from her students and ordinary, everyday life experiences.

Lightning Source UK Ltd.
Milton Keynes UK
UKHW010837150522
403009UK00001B/160